# REIMAGINING OUR MOUNTAINS

**An Ode to SIKKIM and Its Kin: KALIMPONG & DARJEELING**

## Hemant Niroula

INDIA • SINGAPORE • MALAYSIA

ISBN 979-8-89588-322-8

To the splendid mountains of Sikkim, from whose
heights, wisdom and beauty flow.

To the enduring spirit of these peaks, and to the
hearts they've touched and molded.

"Sit down before fact like a little child, and be
prepared to give up every preconceived notion,
follow humbly wherever and to whatever abyss
Nature leads or you shall learn nothing."

**– Thomas Henry Huxley**

# CONTENTS

# INTRODUCTION

Sikkim is my home, and Kalimpong is my maternal grandparent's home and where I was born. Having lived as a wanderer and a dweller in two different states, Sikkim, and the adjoining hills of Darjeeling and Kalimpong districts of West Bengal, I have gathered over the years a personal perspective on the mutating mountain life over time and across various situations which may or may not resonate with every individual, as all experiences are unique from one another.

I grew up in a time when academics were widely considered the ultimate goal in life. The trend of becoming an academician in school followed in Sikkim after it joined India in 1975 when jobs and money flooded the economy. Sikkim in the early 20th century had very few decent schools, as most parts of Sikkim were underdeveloped and underpopulated compared to its neighbours Kalimpong and Darjeeling. The British, who oversaw the flat lands of India, also had their eyes on the cool hills of

Kalimpong and Darjeeling and took them away from Bhutan and Sikkim in the mid-19th century during their era of expansionism and industrialism.

The hills of Kalimpong and Darjeeling were more than just scenic spots for the British. They used them as their getaway places for relaxation, away from the heat and dust of the plains. They set up tea gardens, power plants, and schools in the hills as part of their plan to grow their industry and influence. But their main goal was to reach Tibet through Kalimpong, using the Jelepla Pass as a shortcut. They wanted to trade with Tibet and get access to their rich resources and culture.

Jelepla was the main gateway between India and Tibet, as more than half of the goods and people that crossed the border went through this pass. It was much easier to travel through Jelepla than Nathula, another pass in Sikkim. Jelepla has a gentle slope and a smooth path, while Nathula is steep and rocky. India and China had a border clash in 1962 over two disputed regions: Aksai Chin and Arunachal Pradesh. China declared victory and shut down the Jelepla Pass, which was an important route for trade and travel between India and Tibet. Tibet, which had its own history and culture, was annexed by China in 1949 after Mao Zedong's Communist Party defeated the Nationalist Party of China in a civil war. Mao's policies such as the Great Leap Forward and the Cultural Revolution brought a lot of suffering and death to millions of people, who were forced to give up their homes and traditions.

At the foothills of Darjeeling, at Sidrapong, one of the oldest hydroelectric power stations in India was built in 1897, making Darjeeling the first town in the country to be illuminated by electricity. Darjeeling shone with light, while Sikkim, cloaked in darkness, gazed at it with wonder and admiration from the other side. The old folks of Sikkim, who endured hardships before annexation by India in 1975, praised the Queen of hills, Darjeeling, as a sight as beautiful as the starry night sky. They admired its beauty, culture, and development, as it was the first town in India to have a municipality, a railway, and a hydroelectric power station. They would stop on a hill after a long day of hauling their farm produce towards Darjeeling. They travelled in a caravan, carrying oranges, ginger, butter, and large cardamoms from various villages of Sikkim. They climbed and descended the hills, barefooted, crossing rivers to trade their produce in the bustling market of Darjeeling. After their successful venture and money in their pockets, they would stay for a day or two to enjoy the lively and vibrant atmosphere of the cosmopolitan town. They would take a ride on the toy train and marvel at the scenic beauty of the hillsand valleys and get mesmerised by the splendour of Darjeeling's exquisite tea gardens. They would witness the sunrise, creating a spectacular display of changing colours on the snow-capped peaks of Sikkim from the Tiger Hill viewpoint. They were especially amused to see the telephones of merchants, who were respectfully addressed as *'Seth ji.'*

The merchants enjoyed a high status among the barefooted village people, who believed that they had a direct connection with Delhi through their phones. They supplied clothing and essentials at more than nominal rates, even after a hard bargain. But the villagers still felt a sense of joy and novelty in their simple and humble lives, as they acquired something new and different from the outside world. They would feel the warmth and happiness of being in a place that was both familiar and exotic, a place that was their home and their dream. After their thrilling excursions, they would load their bags with salt and other essentials and trek back to their villages in Sikkim after days of hardship and adventure. Sugar was a luxury they could live without, but salt was a necessity as it sustained not only their lives but also their livestock.

They faced a constant challenge of finding proper nutritious food, as the grains they cultivated on their farms were hardly sufficient to satisfy their hunger throughout the year. However, during times of scarcity, they relied on foraging and hunting in the wild. Today, a typical mountain diet still comprises foraged food like ferns, bamboo shoots, nettles, flower buds, and tender leaves of trees, which not only have medicinal properties but also offer a unique and delicious taste to those accustomed to them. Life was tough for farming households, where large families faced high mortality rates. A person or child who fell ill had little hope of survival, as medical care was scarce and inaccessible. All they could depend on was their knowledge of herbal medicines that they could gather from their farms and forests. Their homes were made of mud, and their roofs were thatched with dry cogon grass, locally known as *'siru,'* which became leaky after a few years of monsoon rains and posed a fire hazard, too. Their journey and life have been lost in oral history, but they have vital significance to our existence. Darjeeling was in Sikkim's heart, who yearned to be and feel like Darjeeling.

Education in the scenic hills of Darjeeling and Kalimpong has been the cherished dream of most parents who have secured incomes for their children. These hill stations have been the cradle of learning for a few kings, queens, aristocrats, bureaucrats, artists, sports men, and many commoners of today and of history, who came from different parts of the country and abroad, especially from Nepal, Bangladesh, and Bhutan, and spent their student days there.

I did not have the opportunity to attend any of the old British era schools but rather enrolled in a modest boarding school at Kurseong, not far away from Darjeeling. I had no clue at the age of four until I reached a chilly dormitory with rows of metal bunk beds and many children like me in February, just before the spring of 1987. I somehow ended up in a similar kind of environment as those who went to such old schools. It took me a few weeks to figure out that life had changed and had to learn fast, as adults were mostly yelling and whipping kids to make them behave. Most adults then did not have much patience in communicating with children.

It was a rough time to grow up, and it became even harder living under absolute strangers during the fading of the violent agitation of the 1986 Gorkhaland movement and before the establishment of the Darjeeling Gorkha Hill Council (DGHC) in 1988. Hundreds of people died in the violence, and the trauma hardened and numbed people in most aspects of life, contradicting the culture and tradition of the hills that cherished sensitivity and resilience. Sunday baths were an ordeal. All children, regardless of gender, stood in a queue naked in the chilly weather of Kurseong, waiting to be bathed in turns. Around three ladies were assigned the task of giving baths. One sprinkled water and sparsely applied soap, the second one scrubbed the skin with a coconut jute until it turned red and sore, and the last lady rinsed the body. Another agony awaited the boys, as their soapless scrotum got scarred due to the friction between the coconut jute and the contours of the delicate hanging tissue, when it got scrubbed. The green-tubed 'boroline' antiseptic cream always came in handy during such incidents to pamper the unpampered.

The British had left a lasting influence on their former subjects: they continued to treat each other with the same perspective and behaviour that they had endured during the colonial era; people subconsciously learned their colonial ways and methods of treating each other as a sign of superiority, rather than trying to understand their validity or morality.

After spending five years at Kurseong, I moved to Kalimpong to attend a Scottish missionary boarding school, Dr. Graham's Homes, on a hilltop for two years. Sharing space with students from various states and abroad, mostly from Nepal, Bangladesh, and Bhutan, was an overwhelming experience. Sports such as hockey, baseball, rugby, lawn tennis, swimming, and boxing were also played as well as other competitive games such as football, basketball et cetra that are played among schools. Sometimes, a few of us sneaked out of the classroom from the back door without being noticed, or perhaps the teacher was lenient towards us few. We caught glistening dragonflies over the meadow near the school toilet by throwing sweaters on them like fishers; and transformed them into our pets by tying a long thread to their tails and letting them soar while holding on to the other end.

We played marbles and whirling tops, locally known as *'lattu,'* vigorously. We also dug trenches and made small bunkers by weaving the long stalks of the Christmas flower plant to play war games in the forest near our cottage. Life had changed dramatically, from the restrictions of Kurseong to the adventures of Kalimpong, from the absence of melodies in life to harmonising the famous John Denver song *'Take me home, country roads'* in a choir on a grand piano during music classes.

Living in the school's dilapidated residential cottage, Assam, keeping oneself clean was not a priority. A splash on the face and rare baths were enough to get by, owing to the shortage of water supply. Water shortage was and still is a big issue not only in schools but also in many areas of Kalimpong. Water is a daily concern, and *'Bagh Dhara,'* one of the major freshwater sources of Kalimpong, has been a lifeline for most areas of the town for ages while the other areas still suffer the shortage. Similarly, Jorethang is one such town in Sikkim with a severe water crisis. The lack of water and the summer heat of Jorethang, which can reach up to 40°C, make life very hard for the people. Only a comprehensive and sustainable plan for clean water supply management can transform these towns from a stagnant economic state to a more dynamic one.

Water scarcity has also created another problem of garbage accumulation in an environmentally challenging situation that our world is facing today. Many restaurants and fast-food outlets are compelled to use disposable cups and plates to serve their customers to save water. However, these disposable items, which are mostly made of plastic, are not easily biodegradable and cause a lot of pollution. The amount of garbage produced by these towns daily is excessive and often ends up in landfills or water bodies, where they can harm wildlife and the ecosystem. The lack of clean water and the increase in garbage have resulted in poor hygiene, the spread of diseases, and the deterioration of public health.

After seven years of living in the hills of Kurseong and Kalimpong, I returned to Gangtok, home, for a pit stop. I must have needed an extensive overhaul after living in the confined wilderness of boarding schools. I joined a school near my home, where I enjoyed two years of comfort and convenience. However, I also faced a barrage of homework assignments, which I failed to cope with. I flunked class six and had to leave the comfort and conveniences. My fate then took me to another boarding school, St Xavier's, at Pakyong, where I spent the next six, finest, years, without flunking again. My transition from the preschool of Geyzing to Kurseong, Kalimpong, Gangtok, and Pakyong within a span of ten years was a difficult journey of adjusting to changing places, people, and friends.

An institute is not built around the likes and dislikes of an individual. It is built around a system of discipline where everyone must follow, and boarding schools are such an environment of 24 hours of discipline. A home is the only place where one can find one's comfortable space, and people to unwind the day and balance out the day's stress. A boarding school is more like an industrialised human farm that offers benefits in terms of various activities that are not conveniently available at home, such as more time for games and stage activities. However, the children living in a boarding farm are worse than sheep, for they are only engaged in the activities within the farm, remaining experientially away from the variety and diversity of one's real world outside. Relationship building and diverse social interaction and experiences are almost cut off daily, which are supposed to be vital as one grows up when the eventuality of every person is to return back to the real world from the bubble of limited experience of boarding schools.

After finishing school, Bangalore took four years to pursue graduation and exploration. I had the privilege of travelling to remarkable places in Karnataka, Tamil Nadu, and Andhra Pradesh, along with my parents, grandfather, and friends. Coming out from an institutionalised life of boarding schools to experiencing the liberating air of freedom, keeping freedom for life became an apparent choice to live and learn. With an amalgam of honesty and care I present to you this booklet, Reimagining Our Mountains.

# THE PROPHECY

An area of 7096 square kilometres and a population of less than seven lakhs, Sikkim is home to diverse hill cultures who share common beliefs in preserving its environment and its social harmony. The environment, terrain, and its natural resources play an important role in shaping the very fabric of Sikkim's social structure and attitude towards life. Every culture and tradition in the world has a distinct identity and significance, which has been inspired by its local habitat. Sikkim's culture reflects a unique blend of different customs, languages, festivals, arts, crafts, food, and music, influenced by its history and geography. Our ancestors, with their use of creative intelligence and the available resources, have come a long way from being hunters and gatherers to become industrious, and by sharing and passing down their knowledge, traditions have evolved and withstood the test of time. .

Before the establishment of a kingdom, Sikkim remained isolated from the world, inhabited by few people belonging to various tribes and traditions. But all had one commonality of belief in animism. Animism is the belief that natural objects, phenomena, and the universe itself possess souls or consciousness. Revering and worshipping nature and not overutilising it has been the backbone of almost all the hill traditions. This sacred bond with nature has preserved Sikkim's rich biodiversity, a stark contrast to the modern methods of overexploiting nature that have wrecked our planet's ecology and inflicted distress and new diseases on every form of life.

In the 8th century, Guru Padmasambhava, also known as Guru Rinpoche, came to Sikkim along with his disciples for a long spiritual retreat. According to various religious texts, Sikkim is regarded as a sacred land of pilgrimage and a place of meditation and dharmic practice. Guru Padmasambhava blessed and sanctified the land and its water bodies with his miraculous powers and meditated in caves. He also concealed many hidden teachings *(Terma)* in Sikkim for the benefit of future seekers. The four holy caves where he stayed and meditated are located around the

Tashiding monastery in its four directions: north, south, east, and west. These caves are known as *Sharchog Bephug, Lho Ngo Phug, Nub Dechen Phug,* and *Jang Lhari Nyingphug.* They are prominent places for pilgrims who seek the blessings of Guru Padmasambhava. One can reach these caves by walking from a few hours to days. Legend says that Guru Padmasambhava transformed evil spirits and goblins into benevolent ones and instated them as guardians of the mountains and its people.

He then made an important prophecy after his meditations, that centuries later a monarch upholding the laws of Dharma would be established in Sikkim. Hence, true to his foretelling, the kingdom of Sikkim was founded in the year 1642 at Yuksom, after eight hundred years of the said prophecy. A man named Phuntsog Namgyal, belonging to a priestly family who was said to be churning milk for butter at his residence in present-day east Sikkim, was chosen by three monks who came from different directions from Tibet to establish the new kingdom. With the collective support of almost all the ethnic tribes, a simple man was consecrated as the first King of Sikkim. He was crowned as the first *Chogyal* or Dharma King of Sikkim, and built the first monastery in Sikkim, the Dubdi Monastery, at Yuksom. On the foundations of Peace and Dharma, Sikkim began its journey as an administration.

# A BRIEF STORY OF ECONOMICS

Economic activity is the art of creating value and convenience for human life, where people in a society collaborate to contribute to the common welfare of one another by offering services or goods in return for payment or by generosity to keep human civilisation advancing. Economic activity has its roots in the establishment of a family, a community, and then communities belonging to various social groups encountering one another. It led to the cultural exchange of goods, services, and ideas, enriching life with diversity and innovation. Before the Industrial Revolution, most societies throughout the world relied on agro-pastoral activities for their livelihood and had a similar quality of life. However, lifestyle, clothing, food habits, dwellings, and forms of art varied from place to place depending on the climate and local habitat of different regions. For example, people living in colder climates wore warmer clothes made of wool or fur, while people living in warmer climates wore lighter clothes made of cotton or linen. Road connectivity enabled the bartering of services and goods between people that were unique and useful to one another. People living near the sea traded fish and salt with people living in the mountains who traded wool and herbs. With exposure to a variety of conveniences, people improved their quality of life and experienced a steady rise in population.

As the population and life expectancy increased over the years, the system of bartering became complicated and inefficient. Bartering is the direct exchange of goods and services without using money as a medium. People had to find someone who had what they wanted and wanted what they had, which was not always possible. The diversity of items that people required daily also made bartering difficult, as the shelf life of goods varied, and people often had different preferences and needs. For example, in a small town, a baker wanted to have a kilogram of chicken from a butcher in exchange for three loaves of bread, but on the other hand the butcher did not want bread; he wanted noodles instead. In such circumstances, bartering became time-consuming and wasteful of produced goods, as people had to search for suitable trading partners and negotiate the terms of exchange. Hence, to overcome this economic stagnation and wastage, our ancestors came up with an ingenious idea and invented money. Money became a common and versatile medium that everybody could conveniently carry and exchange for goods and services.

Money has taken different forms since its inception, from natural objects like seashells, stones, and metals to manufactured ones like coins, paper money, plastic cards, and digital currencies. Money became prominent when people began to mint coins made of various metals such as copper, iron, gold, silver, bronze, etc., which had to be processed and extracted from different mineral ores. Minting coins, just like manufacturing any other good, also required a great deal of time, resources, labour, and craftsmanship. Depending on the quality of work and metal, the value was assigned to each coin accordingly. But unlike any other good, money had better advantages.

It was durable, giving it a lifetime guarantee of usability.

It gave flexibility in standardising the value of different commodities and services.

It could conveniently be carried in pockets and pouches while travelling to distant places.

It did not require any maintenance, and

Most importantly, it could be added in value.

The invention of money revolutionised and simplified economic exchange, hence becoming the most sought-after commodity in the world. Money gave immense freedom in the market. It sparked the imagination and creativity of our ancestors, which leveraged new inventions and discoveries. Trade and commerce began to flourish around the world with each connectivity and discovery of unfamiliar places. Money gave humans the freedom to pursue new work opportunities to transform sluggish economic activity into robustness. The flexibility and convenience that money provided surpassed the human ability to work extra hard to accumulate more money, and thus, people started becoming busy, giving birth to business in the world.

Money transformed the way people valued wealth and power. It became a tangible representation of one's social status and influence, as well as a potential source of greed and corruption. Throughout the history of human civilisation, alongside the legitimate and ethical ways of earning money, a sinister and condescending method of exploiting naïve humans also emerged, which is widely known as slavery and corruption. Money, on the other hand, became a boon for the retired, who could use it to alleviate the hardships of old age.

After the invention of money, the world became engrossed in producing and consuming goods and services. One's skill, opportunity, and luck in earning different amounts of money or inheriting it thus created a social hierarchy of High class, Middle class, and Lower class. But what can commonly be observed in a larger percentage across different social classes is that there is a noticeable difference in the personal rooms of people living within a household. The one who earns more within a household has more elaborate furnishings and facilities than the ones who earn less or who do not earn. This subtly promotes a modern industrial mindset that equates consuming more with living better, and the younger generation subconsciously adopts this notion as a measure of success. The world today has become an exhausting race, where people are trapped in a cycle of overproduction and overconsumption which has led to a pressing and immediate concern that is threatening our world today: climate change and the environmental crisis that accompanies it. The human civilisation today enjoys the comforts of industrialisation but at a huge expense to our health and environment.

The modern economic mindset has been driven by the need to earn more to cope with the rising standards and habituated living expenses, which have caused the prices of housing, commodities, and services to soar every year. Money, as a tool, has provided immense freedom from scarcity, but the desire for more has disrupted the harmony of living a naturally healthy life. People have been working extra hard, both honestly and dishonestly, churning the ocean of production and consumption. Nobody could foresee the gradual accumulation of adversities our world is facing today, as a result of overexploiting nature for human-centric developments. The relentless pursuit of industrial economic growth has led to the degradation of the natural environment, the depletion of natural resources, and the disruption of the natural balance.

The world today is confronted with multiple challenges, such as climate change, biodiversity loss, pollution, poverty, adulterated consumption, and epidemics. The way out from these webs of adversities may be difficult, but not impossible. When every individual begins to relax, share what can be shared, and practice sensible consumption of goods and services which cause pollution, we could curtail the adversities collectively and contribute towards creating a healthier environment. We could adopt a more sustainable, circular, and regenerative approach to production and consumption, which minimises waste, maximises efficiency and restores natural capital. Living amidst the miracles of creation, between the playful games of the moon and the sun, economic activity began through natural human behaviour to nurture.

# CHILDCARE AND EPIGENETICS

Living in the mountains is a physically demanding task that requires a lot of endurance and resilience. Our ancestors back in the olden times only had the privilege of experiencing the struggles of an inconvenient life. Life was rough, and childcare was overlooked as survival was the main priority. They had to endure harsh weather, scarce resources, and threats from wild animals. They had no access to modern amenities, such as electricity, plumbing, or medicine. They had to work hard from dawn to dusk, farming, hunting, or gathering. It was common and normal back then to be negligent towards children, such as being fed irregularly, with minimal hygiene, and infants often were left in their cradle in their soiled clothes till they slept off after exhaustion from crying while the parents toiled in the fields. Toddlers were shouted upon and smacked right and left to cut short the tantrums. They had no toys, books, or games to play with, only sticks, stones, or mud to play with. Children often grew up in a deprived environment. Life in every dimension was a melancholic struggle for everyone.

A child comes into the world with a tender heart, vulnerable and dependent on others. A newborn child's mind is like a blank slate that is shaped by the world through the interactions and experiences that it receives from its environment. Neuroscience says that during the first few years of a child's life, the growing brain rapidly forms new synapses, the connections between neurons, at a rate of up to a million per second. By age three, the brain grows up to 80% the size of an adult's brain, and by five, it grows up to 90%. The brain also undergoes significant changes in its structure and function, such as the development of the prefrontal cortex, the region responsible for executive functions, such as planning, reasoning, and self-control. The early years of a child's life are, therefore, a critical period for brain development, as they lay the foundation for the child's cognitive, emotional, and social skills. The quality of interactions and experiences that a child receives during its early years shapes the way the child understands and relates to the world. Thus, a child learns to adapt to its surroundings from what it has perceived in its early years, providing either strong or weak foundations for learning, health, and behaviour throughout life.

The early environment influences the child's brain development by affecting the formation and pruning of synapses, the connections between neurons. Synapses are constantly changing in response to experience, a process called synaptic plasticity. When a child is regularly exposed to a friendly environment, the brain regions involved in learning and well-being are strengthened by the formation of more and stronger synapses, which enhance the communication and coordination of brain cells. A friendly environment can include factors such as warm and responsive parental care, stimulating and enriching activities, positive and supportive social interactions, and safe and secure living conditions. But when a child is regularly exposed to an unfriendly environment, the brain development is impaired by the reduction and elimination of synapses, which impairs the communication and coordination of brain cells.

When a child is repeatedly exposed to stressful situations, the child's prefrontal cortex, the brain region responsible for executive functions such as reasoning and learning, is inhibited by the overactivation of the amygdala, the brain region involved in emotional processing and stress response. The amygdala triggers the release of stress hormones, such as cortisol, which can have harmful effects on the brain and the body. A child who is exposed to chronic adversity and neglect may suffer from adverse effects on the developing brain, the immune system, and the endocrine system. These effects can include impaired cognitive and emotional development, increased susceptibility to infections and diseases, and altered hormonal and metabolic functions.

Stress is a natural and inevitable part of life. It is the body's way of responding to any kind of demand or threat... When experiencing stress, the stress response system gets activated. The brain and body become alert, releasing stress hormones, adrenaline, and cortisol. These hormones then increase the heart rate, blood sugar, and blood pressure to combat immediate stress. However, not all stress is the same. Researchers have identified three types of stress response in young children: positive, tolerable, and toxic. Positive stress response is a mild and brief increase in stress hormones that happen during natural challenges, such as going to school, meeting new people, or visiting a doctor for vaccination. This type of stress is normal and healthy, as it helps the child to cope with new situations, develop resilience, and learn new skills. Tolerable stress response is a more severe and longer-lasting increase in stress hormones that occurs during traumatic events, such as natural disasters, parental divorce, or the loss of a loved one. This type of stress can be harmful, but it can be buffered by the presence of supportive and caring adults, who can help the child to recover, heal, and grow. Toxic stress response is a prolonged and excessive activation of the stress response system that occurs in the absence of adequate love and support from caring adults. Children exposed to chronic adversity and neglect, such as abuse, violence, poverty, or parental substance abuse or mental illness, are affected by toxic stress. This type of stress can have devastating and lasting effects on the child's psychophysiological well-being.

When toxic stress is abnormally prolonged, the stress response system remains active even when there is no harm. The child becomes hyper-vigilant, anxious, and fearful, unable to perceive what joy and care are about. Any normal situation can trigger a stress reaction in the child, making it difficult to calm down, relax, or focus. Children deprived of loving care during the early years of life, while their brain, hormonal, and immune systems are developing, face a high probability that the stress response system can remain a permanent part of life.

Neuroscience has proven the fact that activation of stress hormones in early childhood can reduce neural connections in key areas of the brain dedicated to well-being, reasoning, and learning. The brain regions involved in memory, attention, and executive functions, such as the hippocampus and the prefrontal cortex, are particularly vulnerable to the effects of toxic stress, and the regions involved in emotional processing and stress response, such as the amygdala and the hypothalamus, become sensitive to the effects of toxic stress.

The amygdala triggers the release of stress hormones, such as cortisol, which can have harmful effects on the brain and the body. Hence, children who live in a secure and supportive environment are able to focus more on developing their cognitive, social, and emotional skills, while children who live in a deprived and hostile environment are more focused on surviving stress rather than thriving. Childcare is a major concern in rural and underprivileged areas, where children are often left without adequate care and protection. These children are at a higher risk of experiencing toxic stress and its negative consequences. They need more attention, intervention, and assistance from society to ensure their healthy development and well-being.

Elderly people who have witnessed the pre- and post-annexation of Sikkim by India in 1975 recall that children in their olden times were timid, and today they are amazed by the verbal skills of 21st-century toddlers. They attribute this difference to the harsh conditions they faced in their youth when they had to struggle with cattle, poor hygiene, inadequate nutrition, lack of medical care, and an uncertain future. They had little time and attention to devote to childcare. Most children grew up without affection and care, and some succumbed to diseases and neglect. Flogging and shouting were common methods of discipline. Adults used to have the liberty to inflict verbal and physical abuse on children in various contexts, such as schools, homes, hotels, and workplaces, until the Right to Education (RTE) Act was passed in 2009, prohibiting corporal punishment. Having endured similar treatment in their childhood, adults believed that harsh methods were essential to enforce discipline. There is evidence of research that corporal punishment has led to lower IQ, lower self-esteem, higher rates of aggression, delinquency, and anti-social behaviour in children.

Children who grow up with care and those who grow up deprived have stark differences in their well-being. Deprivation affects not only the emotional, social, and cognitive development of children but also their physical health. Children who lack care and support are more likely to suffer from illnesses and visit the doctor frequently, compared to those who grow up in a nurturing environment. One of the main causes of illnesses in both children and adults is chronic stress, which impairs the immune system's function. Chronic stress makes the body prioritise energy for the fight or flight response to stress and reduces its ability to fight off infections. Stress hormones, such as adrenaline and cortisol, are naturally produced by the body in small amounts to help regulate blood pressure, blood sugar, and cope with stress. They are especially useful in the morning to activate the body for the day. However, when the body produces too much of these hormones on a regular basis, they can harm the body's health. Excessive stress hormones can weaken the immune system, raise the heart rate, blood pressure, and blood sugar, and eventually cause various diseases. Some of the common diseases linked to stress are hypertension, diabetes, heart problems, depression, anxiety, brain haemorrhage, gastrointestinal issues, and many more.

Stressful childhood experiences can have lasting effects on adult health. Adults who have faced trauma, abuse, neglect, or violence in their childhood are more likely to develop chronic diseases, such as hypertension, diabetes, heart problems, brain haemorrhage, and gastrointestinal issues. These diseases are becoming more common every year, affecting millions of people worldwide. Stress also causes serious mental health problems, such as depression and anxiety, which can impair a person's functioning and well-being. Depression and anxiety can lead to harmful behaviours, such as substance abuse, suicide, and crime, which can further damage the individual and the society. Our society has been suffering from the negative effects of stress for a long time, and it is not easy to break this cycle. It would require a lot of time, investment, and persuasion to educate people about the causes and consequences of stress, and to provide effective help to those who need it most.

Diseases that have been acquired have the ability to get transmitted across generations through the memory and information encoded in the genes. Genes are the units of heredity that carry information from parents to offspring. The Human Genome Project, which was a global effort to map all the genes in humans, estimated that humans have about 20,000 to 25,000 genes that code for proteins. Proteins are the building blocks of life that perform various functions in the body. To understand how genes work, let us take an example of a gene that affects the eyes. Suppose there is a gene, called gene A, which is involved in the development of human eyes. Gene A can have different forms, called alleles, which can influence the eye colour, shape, and health. Each parent has two copies of gene A, and they pass on one copy each to their child. The child's eye features depend on the combination of alleles they inherit from their parents. For example, if both parents have blue eyes, the child will also have blue eyes. But if one parent has brown eyes and the other has blue eyes, the child may have either brown or blue eyes, depending on which allele is dominant, and in rare cases, some have two differently coloured eyes. Similarly, if one or both parents have an eye disease, such as glaucoma, the child may also inherit the risk of developing the disease later in life. Therefore, gene A determines the eye features and physiology of the child by combining the information from both the parents.

Genes are the parts of our cells that store all the important information about us, like a computer program that runs a machine. They tell our cells what to do and how to grow. They also carry information that can make us sick or healthy, by having different versions that we inherit from our ancestors. Some versions of genes are good for us, and some are bad for us. When we are born, we get one copy of each gene from our mother and one copy from our father. The combination of these copies determines what information is expressed in our body. For example, if we get a bad version of a gene from one parent that can cause a disease, and a good version of the same gene from the other parent that can prevent the disease, then we may or may not get the disease, depending on which version is stronger. The stronger version is called dominant, and the weaker version is called recessive. If the bad version is dominant, then we are more likely to get the disease, and if the good version is dominant, then we are less likely to get the disease.

But inherited genes are not the only thing that affects our health. Our environment and behaviour can also influence our genes. Epigenetics is the study of how our genes can be turned on or off by changing the way they are packaged in our cells. Our genes are made of a long molecule called DNA (Deoxyribonucleic Acid), which is wrapped around proteins called histones. The DNA and histones together form a structure called chromatin. The chromatin can be modified by adding or removing chemical groups, such as methyl or acetyl groups. These modifications can change how tightly or loosely the DNA is wrapped around the histones, and how accessible it is to the human machinery that reads the information. When the DNA is tightly wrapped, the gene is turned off. When the DNA is loosely wrapped, the gene is turned on. These changes do not alter the DNA sequence, but they affect the gene expression.

The environment and behaviour of a person can cause changes in their chromatin. For example, smoking cigarettes or eating unhealthy food and leading a stressful life can add more methyl groups to their DNA, which can turn off some beneficial genes. This can increase their risk of getting diseases, such as cancer, diabetes, or heart problems. On the other hand, living in a clean area, exercising regularly, or eating healthy food can remove some methyl groups from their DNA, which can turn on some beneficial genes. This can reduce their risk of getting diseases and improve their health and well-being. Therefore, the genes of a person are not their destiny. They can influence their genes by their choices and actions. For example, having a parent who has diabetes can increase their chance of inheriting a defective version of a gene that can cause diabetes. But they can lower their chance of getting diabetes by changing their lifestyle, such as exercising more, eating less sugar, and avoiding stress. By doing this, they can turn off the defective gene and turn on the functional gene and lead a healthier life.

Stress is a powerful environmental factor that can affect the expression of genes in the cells of the adrenal glands, which produce stress hormones such as cortisol and adrenaline. These hormones regulate the body's response to stressful situations, but when they are chronically elevated, they can cause harmful effects on the body and mind. Research has shown that stress can alter the epigenetic mechanisms that control gene activity, such as DNA methylation and histone modification, making some genes more or less active than they should be. This can lead to changes in the structure and function of the brain, the immune system, the cardiovascular system, and other organs and tissues. Moreover, these epigenetic changes can be inherited by the next generation, increasing their vulnerability to stress and its related diseases.

The first few years of life are a critical period for the development of the brain and the body, as well as for the formation of personality and identity. During this time, the brain is highly plastic and sensitive to the environment, forming millions of neural connections every second. The quality and quantity of the interactions that children have with their parents, caregivers, and peers, as well as the stimulation and support they receive from their surroundings, can shape their brain architecture, and influence their cognitive, social, emotional, and physical development. When children are exposed to positive and nurturing experiences, they can build a strong foundation for learning, health, and well-being throughout their lives and, when exposed to negative and stressful experiences, such as violence, abuse, neglect, poverty, or discrimination, they can suffer from developmental delays, impairments, and disorders that can affect them in the short and long term.

It may take generations to eradicate chronic diseases that are influenced by stress and its epigenetic effects by creating a healthy and supportive environment for children to grow and thrive. The future of our society depends on the actions we take today to ensure that every child has the opportunity to reach their full potential.

The inheritance and creation of wealth have been given a higher priority in our economic policies, but less attention has been paid to the development of a sensible and kind society that values and respects the rights and needs of every individual. No one can predict what a child will become when they grow up; we can only provide them with the best possible start in their early years of life when their brain, organs, and immune system are developing, making its foundations for life. The only choice within the capacity of adults and authorities is to provide a nurturing environment for children and create a healthy environment for generations to come.

# THE ELECTION DRAMA

**"Buy me a month's ration and my family's votes are yours."**

The election is a spectacle of human creativity and drama. In towns and cities, working-class people who have a stable income are not interested in the excitement of the election and have already made up their minds about their preferred candidate. The candidate goes from door to door, greeting the voters with a 'namaste' and handing them boxes of sweets as a token of gratitude and request for their support. The candidate does not linger but moves on quickly to the next house. Some lucky voters who live in towns but have their votes registered elsewhere also receive the boxes of sweets.

The slogan 'The Biggest Festival of Democracy' has been endorsed by the government for the elections pan-India. But not all places experience the same level of excitement and drama during this time. In urban areas, where life is convenient and comfortable, the election is just another event that comes and goes. People cast their votes with little fanfare and return to their routine. But in rural areas, where life is hard and dull, the election is a rare opportunity to celebrate and participate. As soon as the candidates are announced by the parties, the festivities begin. The candidates and their supporters become the hosts and entertainers of the festival, and they use various methods to woo their voters depending on the location and demography. They organise rallies, speeches, songs, and distribute gifts and promises. It is the once-in-five-years festival that the rural population eagerly awaits and enjoys. They know that this is the only time they matter and are heard, and they make the most of it.

For a low-income family relying on government-subsidised ration, having meat twice or thrice a month is a luxury. Many such families do not bother to cook their meals at home during the elections and depend on the food provided by the parties at the canvassing camp. They feast on meat from morning till night and still have the nerve to complain about its taste. Alcohol and elections are like two inseparable lovers that are hard to part, no matter how strict the election rules are. During the olden times there used to be a secret recipe to win over the voters by mixing sugar in their drinks on the eve of the polling day. The sugar makes the drink more appealing and intoxicating, making the voters addicted to it. They wake up the next day with a severe headache and a parched mouth and have a vague memory of anything, except that they had a wonderful time with their host, who has given them a night to cherish. And that's how they determine for whom to vote.

The party and the public are caught in a precarious situation where the public wants to feel valued, and the party does everything in its power to maintain their value until the polling is over. In such a scenario, the party manifesto has little value and becomes a coaster for drinks to be served on. The expenses during the election exceed the allocated budget. Taxi owners earn more than three times the amount they normally earn in a day and become the kingmakers of the election. One can easily guess the winning candidate by counting the number of vehicles following a party. There is fierce competition among strong party contenders to pay higher taxi fares than each other. The taxi owners become the shepherds, and the public the sheep. Villagers who seldom get much opportunity to travel seize this chance with utmost joy to travel wherever they are taken for free and relieve their boredom of everyday life. They enjoy the scenic views, the fresh air, and the snacks. The mechanical force of money operates at its peak during elections, and after the elections are over, the economy of the villages plummets to the lowest point. The money dries up, the parties disappear, and the villagers are left with nothing but memories. The human desire to earn is legitimate, and when opportunity knocks on the door of deprived areas, most people grab it by whatever means to stay profitable. Keeping up with the demands becomes a lavish affair.

The spectacle of planting flags on the houses and lawns of voters is another amusing sight to behold. The party workers, accompanied by their candidate, often visit houses of voters that display an opposition flag. They then summon the members of the house for support, and, after exchanging hesitant handshakes, they remove the opposition flag and replace it with theirs, which look brighter and larger than the houses from afar. Such incidents have divided families, and members of a large family join different parties, and their arguments at home never cease. The transition of politics from a public matter to a domestic one happens in no time in rural areas.

The pace of projects for the economic development of villages is also affected by the methods of lavish canvassing. To satiate the demands of voters, the party uses tactful methods to keep the voters temporarily happy. Keeping up with the demands of the festival requires good financial assistance, and the corporates, usually contractors and businesspeople, come forward as sponsors to serve the needs. Some collectively sponsor ration, beverages, vegetables, fruits, chickens, pigs, goats, and buffalos, and some provide monetary assistance to keep up with the growing demands. The wily corporates place their bets depending on the popularity of a party, but in uncertain situations, they secretly support other parties too to remain on good terms with whoever comes to power. This lavish help creates a binding relationship between the party and the corporates that is tacit in nature.Such bonding of obligatory relationships could have been good if it prudently worked towards progress, but in most cases, it has turned out to be parasitic.

The corporates who then get public projects after the government is formed become complacent towards completing the project on time. They delay the work, inflate the costs, and compromise the quality. Paving and carpeting a road, approximately 20 kilometres long, connecting smaller towns through villages takes more than 15 years to complete. It is a road that never ends and a road that never begins. Village children who were going to secondary school when work had commenced reach well into their mid-thirties, struggling to find employment or create employment opportunities for themselves. They grow up seeing the same unfinished road. For any public work getting delayed for an extended period, the next phase of development is hard to come by on time. The people living in such areas are directly affected and are denied the chance to create better livelihood opportunities and claim a better life. They are trapped in a cycle of poverty, dependency, and disillusionment.

Mr Sridhar (name changed), a thirty-five-year-old postgraduate of one such village, Bermiok West

Sikkim, had to go through a painful separation with his government-employed nurse girlfriend who had come as a staff in a government-initiated vaccination drive in schools to his village in 2016. He had met her a year ago at a hospital in Gangtok. He had fallen in love with her and proposed to her. She had accepted his proposal, and they got engaged. But after a year, when she visited his village for the vaccination drive and found out that there was never a clear road to Mr. Sridhar's house, she changed her mind. She could not imagine living her life in such a place, where the only way to reach his house was by walking for hours. She had hoped for a better life, with a decent house. And after careful thought, she decided to call off their engagement. He tried to convince her, but she was firm. He was left with nothing but a broken heart, a ring, and a scar.

When public work is neglected and delayed, it affects the lives of the people who depend on it. They lose their opportunities to improve their skills and earn a decent life. They become frustrated and hopeless as they grow older and see no change in their situation. A generation gets wasted to such an extent that the next generation will have nothing much to look up to and learn from. The cumulative effect of unemployment and the negative outcomes, such as drug abuse and crime, has certainly been bringing harm to stability, peace, and progress. Unemployment leads to poverty, which leads to desperation, crime, and violence. Drug abuse becomes a way to escape from reality, but it also causes health and social problems. These issues undermine the stability, peace, and progress of society and create a vicious cycle of underdevelopment and misery.

The elections are a solemn duty of the citizens, a way to exercise rights and choose leaders. But the elections have become a festival, a spectacle, a carnival. The people are lured by the illusion of the lights, the sounds, the gifts, and the promises. They fall into the trap of the corporates, who act as sponsors and use it as leverage to avoid their responsibility for public works. They take advantage of the people's ignorance and greed and make them dependent on their handouts. Many of the people who enjoyed the sponsorship have no voice to protest the delayed work. Declaring the elections to be a festival misleads the deprived areas, straying from the prime agenda of electing a government that can serve better.

ROAD CONSTRUCTION
WEST SIKKIM
YEAR OF COMMENCEMENT 2012
AGREED YEAR OF COMPLETION 2017
ELECTION 2024

# TIME ZONE

**"Early to bed early to rise makes a man healthy, wealthy, and wise."**

The Indian standard time (IST) is the official time zone of India, which is used for all purposes throughout the country. The IST is based on the longitude of 82.30 degrees east, which is a vertical line that passes through the central part of India. This line crosses through several states, such as Uttar Pradesh, Madhya Pradesh, Chhattisgarh, the northern part of Odisha, and the eastern part of Andhra Pradesh. The IST is 5 hours and 30 minutes ahead of the Coordinated Universal Time (UTC) or the Greenwich mean time (GMT), which is the standard time of the world. This means that when it is 12:00 noon in UTC or GMT, it is 5:30 pm in IST. The IST is the same for the whole country, even though India spans over two time zones. This means that the sunrise and sunset times vary across different regions of India, depending on their distance from the IST meridian.

The world is spherical in shape, and it is divided vertically by 360 imaginary lines called meridians that run from the North Pole to the South Pole. These meridians are also called longitudes, and they are measured in degrees, minutes, and seconds. Each degree of longitude is equivalent to 15 degrees of Earth's rotation, which takes 24 hours or 1440 minutes to complete its day and night cycle. Therefore, each degree of longitude takes four minutes to rotate towards the sun (1440 minutes divided by 360 degrees = 4 minutes). The meridian that passes through Greenwich, England, is chosen as the standard meridian, zero degrees, or the prime meridian for determining the longitude and time of different places around the world. This is because Greenwich was the site of the Royal Observatory, which was the first to use a telescope to observe the position of the sun and other celestial bodies for navigation purposes.

The prime meridian is the reference point for Coordinated Universal Time (UTC) or Greenwich Mean Time (GMT), which is the standard time of the world. The prime meridian divides the Earth into the

Eastern and Western Hemispheres. The countries that lie on the left-hand side of the map from the prime meridian are called the West, and the countries that lie on the right-hand side of the map from the prime meridian are called the East. As the Earth rotates eastward towards the sun, the places that are located in the easternmost part of the globe receive the first sunlight and are one day ahead of the places that are located in the westernmost part of the globe.

Japan is one of the countries that lies in the easternmost part of the globe, and is known as the Land of the Rising Sun because it is among the first to see the sunrise every day. However, no one knows for sure which place on the planet received its first sunlight after the Earth was formed from its early molten state and settled into its orbit. However, by measuring longitudes and maintaining different time zones throughout the world, one can know the time of different locations beforehand and accordingly make travel plans. A time zone is a region on the Earth that has a uniform standard time, usually based on the longitude of the region. There are 24 time zones in the world, each covering 15 degrees of longitude, but some countries and regions use half-hour or quarter-hour offsets for convenience. Thus, setting up standard time zones of different countries facilitated world trade and commerce, as it allowed people to coordinate their activities across different regions and avoid confusion.

The Japan standard time (JST) is 3 hours ahead of the Indian standard time (IST), which means that Japan is 45 degrees east of India in longitude. If it is 11 am in India, then in Japan, it would be 2 pm. Similarly, the sun rises much earlier in the easternmost region of India than in the westernmost region. The difference in sunrise and sunset times between these two regions can be as much as two hours, depending on the season. The crux of the matter is that even though the Eastern states begin their natural day much earlier, all Indian states follow the same standard time, the IST, regardless of the differences in natural day and nighttime.

The IST is based on a longitude of 82.5 degrees east, which passes through Mirzapur, near Allahabad in Uttar Pradesh. This means that the IST is not suitable for the eastern and western parts of India, as it does not match their solar time. During the winters, Sikkim and its neighbouring mountains in the east get dark by five and Gujarat in the west by seven. There is a difference of about two hours of natural daylight time between these two regions. One may wonder why the states lying on the western side of the map from the Indian standard meridian have progressed well in comparison to states on the eastern side. The one crucial reason the Western states have progressed well is due to the privilege of having extra daylight time at their disposal after their schools, colleges, and offices are over for the day. Children taking up any activity get extra daylight time to play and practice more in the Western states, and children in the Eastern states are deprived of it. By the time people reach their homes from schools and offices, it begins to get dark, and they are not able to give time to pursue other activities.

The people in Sikkim and, similarly, its adjoining hills of Darjeeling and Kalimpong have been losing their extra daylight time by beginning and ending their day late. It is because of this simple reason that the Eastern states have remained behind. Research has shown that having a single time zone for India is not optimal, as it affects the productivity, efficiency, and health of the people. Thus, a change in the official timings according to natural day and night time would help in saving energy, reducing carbon emissions, and improving the well-being of the people in the eastern region.

Suppose educational institutions and offices began and ended two hours earlier than the standard official, IST, timings. This change could bring major reforms in the quality of life of people and the dwindling economy of the state. Children coming home early from school would get enough daylight time to pursue and practice other activities of their preference, such as sports, arts, music, or hobbies. They would be able to explore their talents and passions and develop their skills and confidence. Non-academic institutions, such as sports schools, art schools, and music schools, would begin getting better enrollment, as more children and adults would be interested in joining them. This would help such institutions create better-paying employment opportunities for the instructors, coaches, and staff. It would also create a demand for more facilities and equipment, which would boost local businesses and industries. Such activities would also help create a robust and healthy environment for everyone to live in, as they would promote physical, mental, and emotional well-being. People would be happier, healthier, and more productive. The quality of life would become much better if children and adults reached home early from school and work and had more time to do the things they love.

Sikkim is a small Himalayan state where the major source of employment is the government sector, and many such government offices, schools, and colleges are located in villages and suburban areas too. People who go to offices, colleges and schools for work and study in such areas mostly belong to farming families and own small to large farming lands. However, since the owners do not get enough daylight time after their duties, many such farming fields have remained unattended for decades and have either turned barren or into jungles.

The culture, skill, and knowledge regarding local agricultural practices have also been declining with time, making growing and producing our food a difficult task. This has adversely affected the economy and the environment of the state, as well as the health and well-being of the people. Advancing official timings in the state could well prevent such a decline and bring about positive changes. Enough daylight time would allow the people to work on their farm for a longer time than usual, thus producing more food collectively in the state. This would increase food security and the income of farmers, as well as reduce the dependence on imports from other places. Rural employment, tourism, and small businesses related to agriculture would grow steadily, as more people would be engaged in farming and allied activities, such as animal husbandry, horticulture, floriculture, and agro-processing.

With the availability of various kinds of saplings and seeds of fruits, grains, and vegetables in the market, everyone would have the benefit of consuming organically grown produce and remain nutritionally healthy. Sikkim is the first and only Indian state to be known as an organic state due to its implementation of organic farming. Organic farming is a sustainable and eco-friendly way of agriculture that does not use any chemical fertilisers or pesticides but relies on natural methods of pest control and soil enrichment. Organic farming has many advantages, such as improving the soil quality, conserving the water resources, enhancing biodiversity, reducing greenhouse gas emissions, and increasing crop yield and quality. Organic farming also has health benefits, as it produces food that is free from harmful chemicals and rich in nutrients, antioxidants, and phytochemicals. Organic food can prevent or reduce the risk of various diseases, such as cancer, diabetes, cardiovascular diseases, and obesity.

As per the data note provided by the National Family Health Survey (NFHS) 3 (2005-2006), 4 (2015-2016), 5 (2019-2020), nutritional deficiency causing anaemia, wasting, and stunting in children under five years is higher, 25%, in Sikkim than the national average of 20%, and women more than men are also affected by it. Indicating that the people are not getting adequate and balanced diet, which can impair their physical and mental development, as well as their immunity and productivity. A state with healthy people would give an extra edge, as it would improve human capital and the quality of life of the people.

By aligning the official timings with solar time, people would be able to make the best use of natural daylight and the resources available to them. They would be able to balance their work and leisure and pursue their interests and passions. They would also have more time to spend with their families and friends and enjoy the natural beauty and cultural diversity. People would be happier, healthier, and more productive than before, and contribute to the development and prosperity of the state. A timely change in the clock, coordinated with the rhythm of nature, could gently resolve the troubles of health, work, and economy, and reveal the hidden opportunities of possibility.

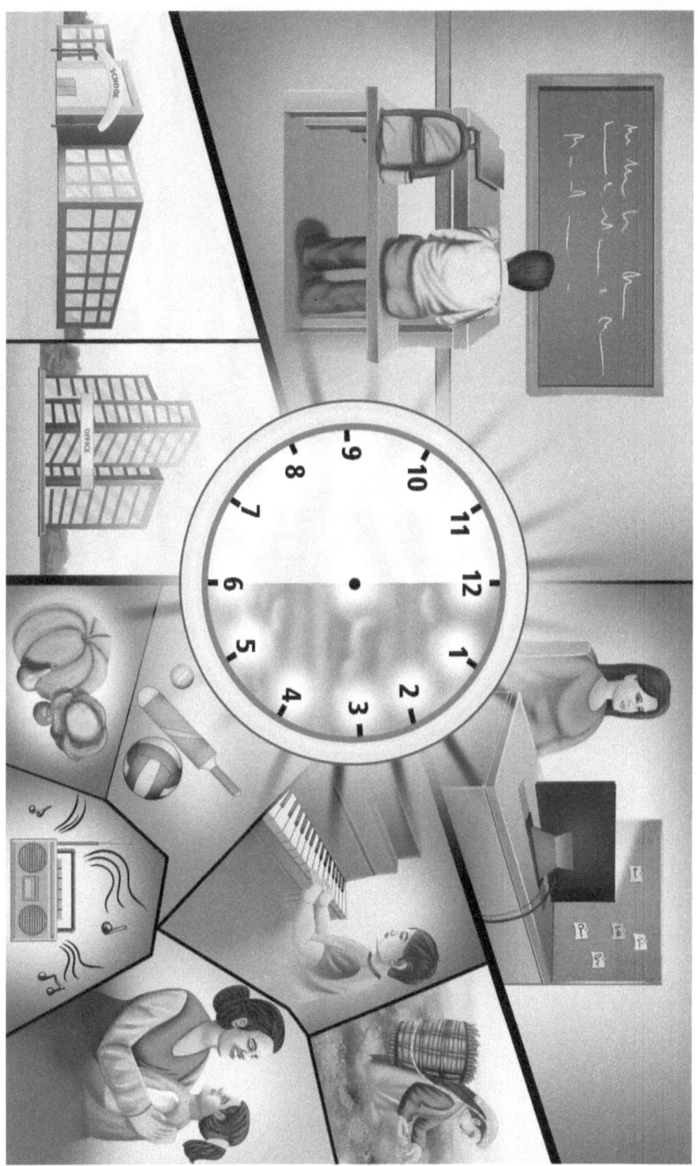
SCHOOL
OFFICE

# MOUNTAIN EQUILIBRIUM AND INDUSTRIALISATION

There used to be a time when common people shared a common work culture that was deeply rooted in the land and the seasons. Farming and occasional hunting were the primary sources of food and wealth creation for the majority of the population. The comforts of innovation in technology, such as cars, radios, and telephones, were only accessible to a few who could afford them during the period of monarchy in Sikkim. These were the symbols of status and power that the common people could only gaze at in admiration and awe.

Under the influence of industrialisation, Sikkim began establishing schools in the late 19th century that focused on modern education methods based on the industrial economic movement of the British Empire. These schools promised to impart new knowledge and skills that would enable the students to compete and succeed in the changing world. A major chunk of the agricultural population began enrolling their children in schools, hoping that it could provide them with comfort and opportunity in the future, which indeed it did for many of them. Sikkim has since then been through major events of economic and political developments since the idea of an industrial economy began taking shape as a global culture. From the mainstream occupation of farming, people began having diverse occupations. People moved from villages to towns and from towns to the cities, seeking better prospects and facilities. The culture, ideas, and economic activity between communities and agriculture thus began declining and brought new social changes with every acquired convenience of industrialisation. The traditional way of life that had sustained the people and the environment for centuries was gradually replaced by a modern way of life that was driven by consumption and competition.

The mountains that had witnessed the hard work and dedication of our ancestors, who used bare hands and iron tools to carve them into terraced fields for farming, have turned barren and into jungles today. The fertile land that once produced abundant crops and supported the livelihoods of the people is now lying idle and overgrown with weeds. With modernisation in infrastructure and better road connectivity, the golden period of Sikkim began and went on for at least two decades after its annexation to India in 1975. Sikkim received more funds and attention from the central government for its development and security. Educated children of farmers began getting jobs in the government, which offered them stable incomes and benefits.

Students of Sikkim then had to sign a bond with the government that upon completing professional and higher studies they had to return to be of service to the government. This ensured that the human capital of Sikkim was not lost to other states or countries. The combination of young, educated job holders and their diligent elders and parents created a healthy and wealthy Sikkim. The balance between the comforts of industrial modernisation and agricultural output was such that a variety of fresh and non-genetically modified local fruits, vegetables, grains, and meat was available and assured to everyone's plate. People enjoyed the best of both worlds, having access to modern amenities and natural resources.

Sikkim lived through joyful times, but now faces the challenges of environmental degradation and food insecurity. Today, when agriculture has taken a back seat, the source of our food is grown and reared with harmful chemicals and is genetically modified to feed our burgeoning population. Government work was available so much so that people had the privilege of choosing jobs of their preference. A matric pass-out could become a primary teacher in a rural school when there was a shortage of qualified teachers. The government provided ample opportunities for employment and education for the people of Sikkim.

With the promise education showed, all children in Sikkim were put to schools from an early age. They were encouraged to pursue higher studies and professional courses that would open up more doors for them. As a result of this, everyone today is on the hunt for better-salaried jobs. However, this also means that the competition for jobs is higher, and the demand for skills is more diverse. One of the perils of the 21st-century generation is that most do not have the skills of farming and manual labour and, at the same time, do not have their choice of jobs in a desired place. They are caught between the aspirations of a modern society and the realities of a mountain state.

Before the Indian economic reform of 1991, the government had authority over the regulation of the market economy and private industries. The people working for and with the government were getting wealthier, while the government was getting poorer owing to careless managerial practices and the rise in crude oil prices in 1990, which was being imported from the war-stricken Gulf. The country was going through a rough time, while Sikkim, with its manageable agrarian population, was not affected. The newly acquired Himalayan state was being funded by the central government for further infrastructural development, as it was necessary to strengthen its international bordering areas.

A white-collared government official during the golden period of Sikkim could buy a reasonable plot of land by saving a minimum of a year's salary. Iron, concrete, labour, and land prices were low. Development in Sikkim soared with the mushrooming of concrete buildings that completely changed the dynamics of living standards. People came out from mud-made houses to enter the convenience of concrete houses. Electricity reached most places, replacing kerosene lamps. Televisions and stereos became items of luxury, and people enjoyed their lives to the fullest.

After the economic reform of 1991, when the country adopted the free market system of capitalism, the market flooded with umpteen creative products to lure more consumers. Since then, a consumption-driven economy slowly started becoming a hardwired habit of the newly born modern society. A limited variety of vehicles that used to take more than five years for delivery became easily available with more options in the market. Competition between private companies to lure more consumers created more jobs in states that had a great deal of affordable skills, convenient logistics, and resources for production.

However, Sikkim, being majorly an agrarian and landlocked Himalayan state, could not compete in the new market economy due to the lack of affordable resources and skills for an industrial set-up. Mountainous roads have twists and turns, and the cost of transportation is high compared to the plains. A traffic-free, forty-kilometre road in the plains could be covered within an hour, while a mountainous road would take two hours. Sikkim, being landlocked, thus provided its delicate young mountains and rivers for hydroelectricity and is contributing as *'urja'* and *'shakti'*,(terms for energy) in driving the economy of the country while facing devastating natural calamities due to it.

An agrarian community in Sikkim lived in harmony with nature and depended on the farm and less on the market. Families during the olden times accommodated themselves in sparsely differentiated mud-made houses that blended with the landscape. Family members and guests often gathered, cooked, ate, and slept in a common space, sharing songs and stories. Elders could even be heard getting intimate at night, despite the lack of privacy and comfort. This resulted in people during those times having more than six children, on average, which was also a way of ensuring their survival and support in the harsh conditions. Privacy was minimum, and everybody naturally lived a public life, where social bonds and mutual support were strong.

Modern education, which was introduced in Sikkim, gave rise to a new industrial society that resulted in various forms of pollution and new diseases that have subsequently infested most people's lives. The influence of industrialisation on the community-based approach to life in the mountains has gradually been replaced by values of selfhood, which is a social norm today. Today, the world offers us numerous things to keep ourselves busy and entertained throughout the day, unlike the olden days when agro-pastoral activities were the only occupation that required people to work together and depend on each other. Farming was a way of life that fostered community spirit and mutual support, while money was of secondary importance.

New work opportunities in the urban areas and other sectors lured many people away from their ancestral villages and farms, resulting in a gradual decline of the farming communities and their traditional practices. This is one of the prime reasons for the decline in farming, which has adversely affected food security and the environment. The terraced fields that were carved by the hard work of the ancestors are now lying barren and overgrown with weeds. These fields, which once produced abundant crops and supported the livelihoods of people, are now a testimony of the fading culture and the changing landscape of our mountains.

With the convenience of building concrete structures, people chose the privilege of extra privacy in both homes and offices, having differentiated spaces emphasising more on individualism. The new architectural module copied from the west began having master bedrooms in new homes with elaborate furnishings for the more privileged. The new age homes of an industrial society began having masters who enjoyed the comforts of modern amenities and gadgets. The mountain people that had been habituated to living as a robust community within a village and between villages for centuries have dissipated due to new work opportunities, separating people from one's roots and culture daily.

People left behind their ancestral traditions to pursue their dreams, where they now face new challenges and competitions. Living on the farm sown from the seeds of industrialisation has enhanced life by conveniences but has taken away the nature of life. Pollution, climate change, infertility, corruption, inflation, and new diseases have all come as grand byproducts of industrial conveniences. The modern-day society has been habituated and hardwired to consume more than one's need in an environmentally challenging world. An individual's carbon footprint and the global temperature are rising every year as the world economies are figuring out solutions to curb the emission of greenhouse gases without having to hinder employment and the livelihood of people.

For every one-degree Celsius rise in temperature, the atmosphere has the capacity to hold up to seven percent more water vapour by drying up lakes and melting glaciers. This is because warmer air has more space and energy to accommodate water molecules in the gaseous form. The water vapour comes from two main sources: evaporation from the oceans and lakes, which cover most of the Earth's surface, and the melting of glaciers and ice sheets, which cover a significant portion of the Earth's land area. The water that is produced by melting can either flow into the oceans and lakes or form glacial lakes that can cause floods if they burst. The increase in water vapour content has implications for the climate system, as water vapour is a powerful greenhouse gas that traps heat and enhances the warming effect. The Khecheopalri Lake, situated in West Sikkim, is one such lake that is gradually shrinking in size due to global warming. On the other hand, lakes fed by melting glaciers are swelling in size, increasing the risk of glacial lake outburst floods (GLOFs).

As the climate warms, more water evaporates from the oceans and lakes, increasing the amount of water vapour in the atmosphere. This leads to more frequent and intense storms, which can produce torrential rain, flash floods, and landslides. These extreme weather events can have devastating impacts on the lives of humans and other living beings. The GLOF that happened in Sikkim on 4th October 2023 resulted in at least more than 90 deaths and over 100 missing people, including 22 Army personnel, and cattle buried under the sludge. The flood was caused by the breach of the South Lhonak Lake, a glacial lake located at an altitude of 17,000 feet in Sikkim's northwest, due to heavy rains. This is one such devastation due to climate change. The effects of global warming and climate change are evident, and we are witnessing the upheaval of it.

We are living in a paradoxical era of human history, where the benefits of industrialisation are accompanied by the perils of climate change. On the one hand, we enjoy the comforts and conveniences of modern technology, such as running water, electricity, transportation, and LPG, which have freed us from the drudgery of manual labour and enabled us to pursue other interests and opportunities. On the other hand, we face the existential threats of environmental degradation, resource depletion, and social inequality, which are the consequences of our unsustainable consumption and production patterns. It is time that we need to rethink our relationship with nature and each other and embrace a new way of development that is based on empathy, collaboration, and resilience. Therefore, we need to challenge ourselves to unwire the hardwired and habituated modern culture of futile consumption and adopt a more sustainable way of life that respects the limits of nature and the needs of others.

Sikkim and its neighbouring mountains of Kalimpong and Darjeeling are small but diverse. It is home to the third-highest mountain in the world, Kangchenjunga, which is revered as a guardian deity by the people. The mountains are not only majestic but also rich in biodiversity, as they host a variety of ecosystems, from tropical forests to alpine meadows, and from cold deserts to glacial lakes. It has more than 4,500 species of plants, 700 species of birds, 150 species of mammals, and many other forms of life, some of which are endangered. The mountains also play a vital role in the water cycle and the climate, as they store and release water from snow, ice, and glaciers and feed many of the regions major rivers, Teesta and Rangeet. However, the mountains and ecology are under threat from climate change and pollution. These factors affect the quality and quantity of water, soil, and air, and the health and survival of the living beings that depend on them. The Himalayan ranges, and their mountains are geographically sensitive zones from where water is naturally rejuvenated and flows into the plains, replenishing every form of life. As the quality and quantity of water from the mountains decline, the risks of water scarcity, food insecurity, biodiversity loss, and disease outbreaks have increased for both humans and wildlife.

The mountains have always been a region for retreat where everything is naturally slow-paced. They offer a unique opportunity for spiritual, cultural, and recreational experiences, as well as for learning and innovation. Making the mountains commercially industrious could be futile and harmful, as it would disrupt the delicate balance of nature and society. Instead, by harnessing the talents and physical attributes of the people in areas of sports, agriculture, holistic education, and different forms of art, could foster the quality of life sustainably, economically, and environmentally and become a source of inspiration, innovation, and transformation.